BOONE and WYATT'S

Friends of All Seasons

Terri Braden Monahan

AuthorHouse™
1663 Liberty Drive
Bloomington, IN 47403
www.authorhouse.com
Phone: 1 (800) 839-8640

ISBN: 978-1-7283-1962-9 (sc)
ISBN: 978-1-7283-1963-6 (e)

Library of Congress Control Number: 2019909816

This book is printed on acid-free paper.

Print information available on the last page.

Published by AuthorHouse 07/18/2019

authorHOUSE®

Boone and Wyatt have a window seat to view friends in their backyard. Oftentimes, their view seems more like a picture post card. They have friends of all colors, sizes and shapes. So, in order to see, please open the drapes!

Even though Winter can get rather frozen, this is the home where they stay and the home they have chosen. Perhaps it is because there is food always here and it's comforting to know lunch is always near.

Some winter days may be cloudy and gray, but today is sunshine with snow to have fun in and play!

What are they looking for and what do they need? It's apparent to me they hope to find a black oil sunflower seed!

After the storm, there are tracks in the snow! This leads me to believe we have a Buck and a Doe!

Not everyone's so lucky to have a window seat view, in this I'll confide. But I'll tell you for sure that the birds are much happier when the cats are inside!

Ice storms have a beauty all of their own. Boone and Wyatt are not impressed and are snug in their beds inside their home!

Under the moon, I see opossums and a raccoon. What does the racoon see in the window? Well, it's my cat, Boone! And when I turned on the light...no coon did it fright. You can see things from a window seat even at night!

Spring has arrived and do you know what the Robin has found? Well, an earthworm, with the help of an underground Mole who's busy making tunnels and a nearby mound!

Spring is here but winter still wants to hang around. But this adorable black Squirrel knows where there's seed to be found...and that my friends would be in this backyard and on the ground!

Spring has brought us some lovely Grosbeaks who are headed back north! But I can't tell you how long they will stay here and so forth. In September, they'll need lots of food for their long return trip. I'd be honored to have them use this backyard as their landing strip!

This little Bunny is trying not to be noticed, but I have a feeling she can see the cats in the window who are not hidden, not even in the remotest!

Boone doesn't mind watching today's April showers. The good news is that this rain will soon bring us colorful May flowers!

Oh heavenly Spring, thank you for the longer daylight, the butterflies and the bees. It's lovely to see the grass so green and new buds on the trees!

This female Cardinal is adorable, wouldn't you say? You won't see her ever having a bad hair day...even when it's windy and blowing around, because this bird knows regardless, she has a beautiful crown!

None of these friends feel an alarm. That's because these cats are on their enclosed back porch and can do them no harm!

Summer has brought us a beautiful trio, but only two of the three have spots. That's because this is a Mama and her two babies of which I took a lot of snapshots!

So, when a furry friend finds a seed in a feeder or on the ground, it's clear they are happy with what they have found!

I don't think this Chickadee meant to spit that seed out that was found. You can bet this little bird flies fast and catches that seed before it hits the ground!

Boone and Wyatt can see woodpeckers most any season. It looks like this Downy Woodpecker is doing chin-ups for some reason?!

The Bluebirds inside this house are asking, "What the heck?!" It's because the woodpecker's knock on their door is more of a peck. So please, Mr. Woodpecker, take off with a bound to a place where you are allowed to pound!

The Mr. and Mrs. are dining together. It's a lovely Autumn day to be outside in such weather. We really shouldn't stare as they eat their fair share. So, we'll leave them to their dinner in this backyard of which they think is a five-star winner!

This cutie has hold of some grass rather tight. Whatever her plan, her grasp on the grass is an adorable sight!

With the sun shining on this Cardinal, it's easy to see how he reminds me of an Autumn Blaze Red Maple tree!

Blue Jay, big and blue, thank you for waiting to eat among this crew. It's polite to wait your turn and a lesson I wish everyone would learn! A Blue Jay may look a bit scary, but he is also quite a bit cute. He has a distinctive voice, and it's one that doesn't come with a mute!

Boone and Wyatt are watching this friend eating rather bold, and seem to be wondering how much more can this Chipmunk's cheeks possibly hold?!

A Woodpecker on your porch won't do at all! Please head to your treat brick we've added this Fall! This guy on your house is not really good, especially if your house is made out of wood!

To catch them in flight is harder than you think. Before you know it, they are off in a blink!

This Carolina Wren visits this backyard because there is food. And obviously, it has put him in a good mood. We like this cute little bird and his good attitude!

Sometimes a Goldfinch is bright yellow, and sometimes he is a much dimmer fellow. There's beauty in its every last inch, no matter the color brightness of a beautiful Goldfinch!

Some views are not low on the ground, but high in the sky. Boone and Wyatt have seen rainbows, fireworks, moons, and airplanes. They've seen all of these things and more from inside their window panes!

Someone's in trouble. He's where he should not be! And it's not the Nutcracker, because he *belongs* on the tree! It's time to intervene and time to take notice. This cat needs a time out and time to refocus!

This isn't fair and this isn't nice! Boone knows Wyatt is taking up two beds while dreaming of mice!

Boone and Wyatt have friends from all seasons...of a variety of colors, breeds, and sizes from different regions. Yes, they have quite a friend collection. Their backyard is a diverse selection!

Everyone needs a place to call home... and to have food in their belly and friends so they don't feel alone. You can make a difference by lending a hand, by helping others across our great land!

Sharing is caring, we all know it's true. And I'm happy to say that now you know it too! The world is beautiful and full of different kinds, and of colors, of sizes, ages and interesting minds. Everyone is welcome in our neighborhood...and in this backyard for the common good.

There's a simple rule I'd love you to remember...one that should be observed from January to December. Treat others the way you'd like to be treated, and with this said, my story is nearly completed!

Boone and Wyatt hope you know for many reasons, when speaking of their friends of all seasons...no matter their color, size or their fashion, it's always a good thing to show them compassion!

The outdoor views can't be beat when you are two cats with a window seat!

About the Author

The Author, **Terri Braden Monahan**, grew up on a farm in Indiana, and has loved animals from an early age. Her first book, "*Tuxedo Luke*", was about finding and rescuing her tuxedo kitten. Boone and Wyatt were both rescued from her local animal shelter. One rather long winter, many different kinds of animals came seeking help in her backyard. They needed someone who cared. The same can be true every winter (and every season) for both our animal and people friends. Mrs. Monahan hopes that one day, every single animal and person will have enough food in their belly, a warm bed to sleep in, and of course, friends!

Printed in the United States
By Bookmasters